Billy, the Kid: A Wild West Legend

Copyright Page

TITLE: Billy, the Kid: A Wild West Legend

1ST Edition

Copyright @ 2023

Roberto M. Rodriguez. All rights reserved.

ISBN: 9798223759362

Table of Contents

Billy, The Kid: A Wild West Legend

By Roberto Miguel Rodriguez

Chapter 1: The Life and Legend of Billy, The Kid

The Early Years: Billy's Childhood in New York

In the vast realm of Wild West legends, one name that stands tall is Billy, The Kid. Known for his daring escapades, sharpshooting skills, and his inevitable clash with the law, Billy, The Kid has become an iconic figure of American folklore. But before he became the legendary outlaw, Billy had a humble beginning in the bustling city of New York.

Born on November 23, 1859, as Henry McCarty, Billy spent his early childhood in the teeming streets of New York City. Growing up in a working-class Irish immigrant family, Billy faced the hardships of poverty and the struggle for survival from a tender age. The streets of New York served as his playground and his classroom, shaping the young boy's resilience and resourcefulness.

Despite the challenges, Billy's childhood in New York played a crucial role in shaping his destiny. Inspired by the tales of the Wild West and the adventures of cowboys, Billy developed a fascination for the frontier. He would often spend his days at the local library, engrossed in books about the untamed lands of the West, dreaming of a life beyond the city streets.

It was during these formative years that Billy's love for the Wild West began to take root. He would spend hours sketching cowboys and Native Americans, fueling his passion for art. Billy's vivid imagination transported him to the vast plains of the frontier, where he could feel the freedom and adventure that awaited him.

As Billy grew older, his longing for the Wild West became too strong to ignore. With a heart full of dreams and a thirst for adventure, he left behind his childhood in New York and embarked on a journey that would make him a legend. But his early years in the bustling streets of New York would forever remain a part of his identity, influencing the way he saw the world and the way he would be remembered.

Today, Billy, The Kid's legacy lives on in the hearts of the public. From collectibles and historical tours to art, literature, and movies, the legend of Billy, The Kid continues to captivate the imagination of people across the globe. His story serves as a reminder that even from the most humble beginnings, greatness can be born, and dreams can be realized.

So, whether you're a fan of Billy, The Kid memorabilia, a history enthusiast interested in exploring the Wild West, an artist seeking inspiration, or simply someone intrigued by the legend, take a moment to reflect on the early years of Billy's childhood in New York. It is from this foundation that a legend emerged, forever etching Billy, The Kid's name in the annals of American history.

A Troubled Teen: Billy's Move to New Mexico

In the tumultuous life of the legendary Wild West figure, Billy the Kid, his move to New Mexico stands out as a pivotal moment. This subchapter delves into the events leading up to his relocation, shedding light on the troubled teen's life and the impact it had on his future as a notorious outlaw.

Born in New York City in 1859, Billy the Kid, originally named William Henry McCarty Jr., faced a turbulent childhood. His father's death left him orphaned at a young age, forcing him to navigate a world filled with hardship and uncertainty. As Billy grew older, his rebellious spirit and penchant for troublemaking became increasingly apparent.

At the age of 16, Billy found himself embroiled in criminal activities, leading him to flee to New Mexico in search of a fresh start. The vast, untamed landscapes of the West seemed to hold the promise of a new beginning for the troubled teen. Little did he know that his move to this frontier territory would shape his destiny and contribute to his notoriety.

New Mexico, with its rugged terrains and lawless reputation, provided the perfect backdrop for Billy's transformation into a legendary gunslinger. It was here that he became entangled in the infamous Lincoln County War, a bloody conflict between rival factions vying for economic and political control. Billy's involvement in the war, marked by daring escapes and deadly encounters, earned him a reputation as a fearsome outlaw.

Today, the legacy of Billy the Kid lives on through various mediums, captivating the public's imagination. Collectors seek out Billy the Kid memorabilia and collectibles, eager to possess a piece of Wild West history. Historical tours and sightseeing expeditions offer enthusiasts the chance to walk in the footsteps of the notorious outlaw, visiting key locations associated with his life.

Artists and authors, inspired by Billy's story, have created paintings, novels, and literature that immortalize his adventures. Movies and documentaries further bring his tale to life, captivating audiences with thrilling portrayals of his rebellious exploits. The fashion industry has even embraced the Wild West trend, with clothing and fashion inspired by Billy the Kid and the era in which he lived.

Gaming and video game enthusiasts can also immerse themselves in the Wild West world, experiencing the thrill of being an outlaw like Billy. Photography and vintage photographs offer a glimpse into the past, preserving the visual essence of Billy's time. Additionally, music and songs celebrate his legend, capturing the essence of the Wild West through soul-stirring melodies.

Finally, for those seeking a unique culinary experience, themed restaurants and food establishments offer a taste of the Wild West, allowing patrons to savor the flavors of the era in which Billy the Kid roamed the deserts and plains.

Billy the Kid's move to New Mexico was a turning point in his tumultuous life, propelling him into the annals of Western folklore. Today, his story continues to captivate the public imagination, inspiring a wide range of industries and providing a glimpse into the untamed spirit of the Wild West.

The Lincoln County War: Billy's Involvement in the Conflict

In the annals of Wild West history, few figures loom as large as Billy the Kid. Known for his daring escapades and notorious reputation, Billy's involvement in the Lincoln County War is a chapter that both captivates and mystifies the public. This subchapter delves into the details of Billy's role in the conflict, shedding light on his motivations, actions, and the lasting impact of this tumultuous period.

The Lincoln County War, which took place in New Mexico during the late 1800s, pitted two powerful factions against each other: the Murphy-Dolan faction and the Tunstall-McSween faction. Billy, a young and impressionable teenager at the time, found himself caught in the middle of this bitter feud.

When John Tunstall, a respected English rancher, took Billy under his wing, it marked a turning point in the young outlaw's life. Tunstall's murder at the hands of the Murphy-Dolan faction ignited a fierce desire for revenge within Billy. He joined forces with other members of Tunstall's group, known as the Regulators, and embarked on a series of daring raids and skirmishes against their enemies.

During the Lincoln County War, Billy's cunning and marksmanship earned him a fearsome reputation. He became a symbol of resistance against the corrupt establishment, fighting for justice and avenging the death of his mentor. Billy's involvement in the conflict brought him both notoriety and sympathy, as he became a folk hero in the eyes of the public.

The consequences of the Lincoln County War were far-reaching. Billy's actions, and those of the Regulators, had a profound impact on the region's history. The conflict highlighted the lawlessness and corruption that plagued the Wild West, prompting calls for reform and stricter enforcement of the law.

Today, the legacy of Billy the Kid and the Lincoln County War continues to captivate audiences across various niches. For collectors, there is a thriving market for Billy the Kid memorabilia and collectibles, from authentic artifacts to reproduction items. Historical tours and sightseeing opportunities allow enthusiasts to explore the sites where Billy and his fellow outlaws once roamed.

Artists and authors have been inspired by Billy's story, creating paintings, novels, and literature that capture the spirit of the Wild West and his tumultuous life. The silver screen has also paid homage to Billy, with movies and documentaries bringing his legend to life. Fashionistas can find inspiration in the rugged and iconic style of the Wild West, with clothing and fashion inspired by Billy the Kid and his era.

From gaming and video games to photography and vintage photographs, the allure of Billy the Kid transcends generations, offering a glimpse into a bygone era. And for those seeking a unique dining experience, themed restaurants and food experiences allow patrons to immerse themselves in the atmosphere and flavors of the Wild West.

Billy the Kid, a Wild West legend, left an indelible mark on history through his involvement in the Lincoln County War. His daring exploits and enduring legacy continue to fascinate and captivate audiences across a multitude of niches, ensuring that his name will live on in the annals of American folklore.

Escalation and Infamy: Billy's Notorious Crimes

In the annals of Wild West history, no name stands out quite like that of Billy the Kid. This enigmatic and controversial figure has captured the imaginations of people from all walks of life, becoming a legend in his own right. From the public to niche audiences such as Billy, The Kid memorabilia collectors and Billy, The Kid historical tour enthusiasts, Billy's notorious crimes have become the stuff of legend.

Billy the Kid's criminal escapades began in his teenage years, when he found himself drawn to a life of lawlessness. His first brush with infamy came when he joined a gang of cattle rustlers, stealing livestock from ranches across the New Mexico territory. But it was his involvement in the Lincoln County War that truly propelled him into the spotlight of criminal history.

During the Lincoln County War, Billy the Kid became embroiled in a violent conflict between rival factions, resulting in a series of murders and skirmishes that shook the region. Billy quickly gained a reputation as a ruthless gunslinger, capable of eluding capture and leaving a trail of bodies in his wake. His crimes, often committed in the name of vengeance or survival, made him a feared and wanted man.

One of Billy's most infamous crimes was the killing of Sheriff William Brady. This brazen act of violence solidified his status as a dangerous outlaw and marked a turning point in the public's perception of him. As news of his actions spread, so did the fascination with this young gunslinger, leading to countless works of literature, movies, and documentaries that sought to unravel the mystery of Billy the Kid.

Today, Billy the Kid's legacy lives on in a multitude of ways. Collectors eagerly seek out memorabilia and collectibles associated with his name, while historical tours and sightseeing adventures take enthusiasts on a journey through the places he once roamed. Artists continue to paint his portrait, capturing the essence of his wild spirit, and authors pen novels that delve into the depths of his complex character.

Billy the Kid's impact extends beyond entertainment, as his influence can be seen in fashion inspired by the Wild West, themed restaurants that offer a taste of the frontier, and even video games that allow players to step into his boots. His story has been captured through vintage photographs, while musicians have immortalized him in songs that celebrate his rebellious nature.

Billy the Kid's notorious crimes may have occurred over a century ago, but his legend lives on. Whether you're captivated by his outlaw persona, interested in collecting his memorabilia, or simply curious about the Wild West, there's no denying the enduring appeal of this Wild West legend.

The Outlaw's Demise: Billy's Capture and Execution

In the annals of Wild West history, one name stands out above all others - Billy, The Kid. A legendary figure whose exploits continue to captivate our imaginations today. But every legend has an end, and this subchapter delves into the dramatic events surrounding the capture and execution of this notorious outlaw.

Billy's life had been one of constant danger and lawlessness. His reputation as a skilled gunslinger and his involvement in numerous crimes had made him a target for law enforcement. The authorities were determined to bring him to justice, and their efforts finally came to fruition in the spring of 1881.

It was on a fateful day in Fort Sumner, New Mexico, that Billy's luck ran out. Pat Garrett, the relentless sheriff of Lincoln County, led a posse to apprehend the Kid. The ensuing confrontation was tense and filled with gunfire. In the end, Billy was captured, his reign of terror finally coming to an end.

The public's reaction to Billy's capture was mixed. Some hailed it as a victory for justice, while others mourned the demise of a Wild West legend. The media fanned the flames, sensationalizing every detail of the Kid's capture and subsequent trial.

The trial itself was a spectacle that drew widespread attention. Billy, known for his charisma and charm, captivated the courtroom as he defended himself against the charges. However, the weight of evidence was overwhelming, and he was found guilty of murder and sentenced to death by hanging.

The day of Billy's execution was a somber one, marked by a mixture of curiosity and morbid fascination from onlookers. Crowds gathered outside the prison walls, eager to witness the demise of the Kid. As the noose was placed around his neck, the once-infamous outlaw showed a surprising calmness and stoicism, accepting his fate with dignity.

Billy's execution marked the end of an era. The Wild West had lost one of its most notorious figures, leaving behind a legacy that still reverberates today. The public's fascination with Billy, The Kid, has endured over the years, with countless books, movies, and songs immortalizing his life and exploits.

In this subchapter, we have explored the dramatic events surrounding the capture and execution of Billy, The Kid. From his capture by Pat Garrett to his final moments on the gallows, we have witnessed the downfall of a Wild West legend. Whether viewed as a hero or a villain, Billy's story continues to intrigue and captivate audiences, ensuring his place in the annals of American history.

Chapter 2: Billy, The Kid Memorabilia and Collectibles

Collecting Billy, The Kid: A Historical Perspective

Billy, The Kid is a legendary figure of the Wild West, captivating the imaginations of people across the globe for generations. From his daring escapades to his tragic demise, Billy, The Kid has become an icon of American history. For enthusiasts and fans, collecting Billy, The Kid memorabilia and exploring his legacy through historical tours, art, literature, movies, clothing, gaming, and more has become a passion.

One of the most intriguing aspects of Billy, The Kid's legend is the wide range of collectibles available to fans. From authentic artifacts to replicas, collectors can amass a treasure trove of items associated with this notorious outlaw. Genuine pieces of Billy, The Kid's era, such as his revolver or personal belongings, hold immense historical value and are highly sought after by avid collectors. For those seeking more affordable options, there are numerous replicas available, allowing fans to own a piece of Wild West history.

To truly immerse oneself in the world of Billy, The Kid, historical tours and sightseeing are a must. Exploring the actual locations where Billy, The Kid lived, fought, and ultimately met his end provides a deeper understanding of his life and the times he lived in. These tours offer a unique opportunity to walk in the footsteps of this legendary figure, bringing his story to life.

Art and paintings inspired by Billy, The Kid offer a visual interpretation of his life and adventures. Artists capture the essence of the Wild West through their brushstrokes, allowing fans to appreciate the beauty and excitement of this era. Similarly, novels and literature dedicated to Billy,

The Kid provide an immersive experience, delving into his psyche and the events that shaped him.

For movie buffs and documentary enthusiasts, there is a vast array of films and documentaries dedicated to Billy, The Kid's life. These cinematic works bring his story to the big screen, captivating audiences with thrilling action and emotional depth. Watching these movies and documentaries allows viewers to witness Billy, The Kid's legacy unfold before their eyes.

Fashion inspired by the Wild West and Billy, The Kid's era has also gained popularity. From cowboy hats and boots to fringe jackets and bandanas, this style pays homage to the iconic look of the Wild West. Fans can embrace their inner outlaw by incorporating these fashion elements into their wardrobe.

The world of gaming and video games has not been left untouched by Billy, The Kid's legend. From action-packed adventures to strategic gameplay, these games allow players to immerse themselves in the Wild West and experience the thrill of being a gunslinger.

Photography and vintage photographs offer a glimpse into the past, preserving the memories of Billy, The Kid and his contemporaries. These images capture the essence of the Wild West, allowing fans to witness the faces and places that shaped this iconic era.

Music and songs inspired by Billy, The Kid's life bring the spirit of the Wild West to life through melodies and lyrics. From folk ballads to country tunes, these songs transport listeners back in time, evoking the emotions and stories associated with Billy, The Kid.

For those seeking a unique dining experience, Billy, The Kid themed restaurants and food experiences offer a taste of the Wild West. From hearty cowboy meals to themed decor, these establishments immerse visitors in the ambiance of the era, allowing them to dine like outlaws.

In conclusion, Billy, The Kid's legend continues to capture the hearts and minds of the public. From collecting memorabilia and exploring historical tours to embracing art, literature, movies, fashion, gaming, photography, music, and themed restaurants, there are countless ways to immerse oneself in the world of Billy, The Kid. This subchapter provides a historical perspective on the various avenues available to fans and enthusiasts to celebrate this Wild West legend.

Authenticating Memorabilia: How to Identify Genuine Items

As fans of the legendary Wild West figure, Billy the Kid, we are often drawn to collecting memorabilia associated with his life and legacy. However, with the market flooded with replicas and counterfeit products, it is essential to know how to authenticate genuine Billy the Kid items. In this subchapter, we will guide you through the process of identifying authentic memorabilia, ensuring that you add only genuine pieces to your collection.

1. Historical Documentation: The first step in authenticating Billy the Kid memorabilia is to look for historical documentation. Genuine items often come with certificates of authenticity, letters, photographs, or any other form of documentation that proves their connection to Billy the Kid.

2. Expert Opinion: Seek the expertise of reputable historians, collectors, and appraisers who specialize in Billy the Kid memorabilia. Their knowledge and experience will help you determine the authenticity of an item through careful examination and comparison with known genuine pieces.

3. Provenance and Chain of Ownership: Trace the item's provenance, which refers to its documented history of ownership. Genuine items usually have a well-documented chain of ownership that can be verified through historical records, receipts, or even firsthand accounts.

4. Material and Construction: Pay attention to the materials used and the construction of the item. Genuine memorabilia often exhibits signs of aging, wear, and craftsmanship consistent with the time period in which Billy the Kid lived. Familiarize yourself with the materials commonly used during that era to spot any inconsistencies.

5. Comparison with Authentic Examples: Study authentic Billy the Kid memorabilia through books, exhibitions, or online resources. By familiarizing yourself with genuine items, you can develop an eye for detail, making it easier to identify replicas or fakes.

6. Price and Market Research: Be cautious of suspiciously low prices or deals that seem too good to be true. Conduct thorough market research to understand the typical price range for genuine Billy the Kid memorabilia. If a deal seems too cheap, it is likely a counterfeit.

By following these steps and being vigilant, you can enhance your collection with authentic Billy the Kid memorabilia. Remember, the joy of collecting lies in owning genuine pieces that truly reflect the legacy of this Wild West legend.

Popular Collectibles: Billy, The Kid Artifacts and Relics

In the fascinating world of Billy, The Kid, there is no shortage of captivating artifacts and relics that have captured the imagination of both avid collectors and casual enthusiasts. This subchapter explores the allure of these valuable and historical objects, shedding light on the various avenues through which they have become a cherished part of popular culture.

For fans of Billy, The Kid, collecting memorabilia and collectibles related to this Wild West legend is a passion that knows no bounds. From original weapons and clothing to personal letters and photographs, these artifacts offer a tangible connection to the life and times of this infamous cowboy outlaw. Whether you are a novice collector or a seasoned aficionado, there is a wide range of items available to suit every budget and interest.

For those seeking a more immersive experience, Billy, The Kid historical tours and sightseeing provide an opportunity to step into the footsteps of this legendary figure. These guided tours take you to the exact locations where Billy, The Kid roamed, offering a chance to relive the stories and legends that have made him an enduring icon of the Wild West.

Billy, The Kid's impact extends beyond the realm of history and into the realm of art. Many talented artists have been inspired by his enigmatic persona, resulting in a plethora of stunning paintings and artwork that capture his spirit and mystique. These pieces not only serve as beautiful additions to any art collection but also allow us to delve deeper into the mythology surrounding Billy, The Kid.

Literature and film have also played a significant role in perpetuating the legend of Billy, The Kid. Numerous novels and biographies have been written, exploring different aspects of his life and adventures. Additionally, movies and documentaries have brought his story to life on the silver screen, captivating audiences with thrilling portrayals and dramatic reenactments.

The Wild West fashion inspired by Billy, The Kid's era has also gained popularity, with clothing and accessories paying homage to the rugged charm of the time. From cowboy hats and boots to fringe jackets and bandanas, these fashion items allow us to channel our inner outlaw and embrace the spirit of the frontier.

For those who enjoy gaming and video games, Billy, The Kid-themed options are available, allowing players to step into his boots and experience the thrill of the Wild West firsthand. These virtual adventures offer a unique way to immerse oneself in the legend and excitement of Billy, The Kid's world.

Photography and vintage photographs provide a glimpse into the past, preserving moments in time and offering a visual narrative of Billy, The Kid's life and the Wild West era. These captivating images allow us to witness history through a lens, capturing the spirit of a bygone era.

Music and songs have also been inspired by Billy, The Kid's story. From classic ballads to modern compositions, musicians have found inspiration in his life and exploits, creating a soundtrack that adds depth and emotion to the legend.

Lastly, for those seeking a taste of the Wild West, Billy, The Kid-themed restaurants and food experiences offer a unique culinary journey. From hearty cowboy meals to saloons that transport you back in time, these establishments provide an immersive dining experience that truly captures the essence of the Wild West.

In conclusion, the world of Billy, The Kid collectibles is a vast and diverse one. From artifacts and relics to art, literature, films, fashion, gaming, photography, music, and dining experiences, there is something for everyone to explore and enjoy. So, whether you are a dedicated collector, a curious enthusiast, or simply someone looking to delve into the rich history and mythology of the Wild West, Billy, The Kid collectibles offer a captivating journey into the life and legend of this iconic figure.

Building a Collection: Tips for Aspiring Collectors

Collecting items related to historical figures or events can be a fascinating and rewarding hobby. For fans of Billy the Kid, the Wild West legend, building a collection of Billy the Kid memorabilia and collectibles can provide a unique and exciting glimpse into the life and times of this notorious outlaw. Whether you are interested in Billy the Kid art and paintings, novels and literature, movies and documentaries, or even clothing and fashion inspired by the Wild West, there are plenty of options to explore. Here are some tips for aspiring collectors looking to start their own Billy the Kid collection.

1. Educate Yourself: Before diving into collecting, take the time to learn about Billy the Kid's life, the historical context, and the different types of items associated with him. This will help you make informed decisions and avoid purchasing fake or replica items.

2. Set a Focus: Decide on the specific niche or theme you want your collection to revolve around. This could be paintings, vintage photographs, music, or even themed restaurants and food experiences. Having a clear focus will make it easier to find and acquire relevant items.

3. Research Authenticity: Due to the popularity of Billy the Kid, there are many replicas and fakes in the market. Research and consult experts in the field to ensure the authenticity of the items you are interested in purchasing.

4. Attend Historical Tours and Sightseeing: Participating in Billy the Kid historical tours and sightseeing can provide valuable insights and opportunities to find unique collectibles. These tours often visit historical sites associated with Billy the Kid, giving you a chance to uncover hidden gems.

5. Connect with Fellow Collectors: Join online forums, social media groups, or local collector clubs to connect with other Billy the Kid enthusiasts. Sharing knowledge and experiences with fellow collectors can enhance your understanding and help you discover new items for your collection.

6. Be Patient and Persistent: Building a collection takes time, so be patient and persistent in your search for rare and valuable items. Keep an eye on auctions, estate sales, and online marketplaces to increase your chances of finding unique pieces.

7. Preserve and Display: Once you have started acquiring items for your collection, make sure to properly preserve and display them. Use archival-quality materials and consider investing in display cases or frames to protect and showcase your collection.

Building a collection related to Billy the Kid allows you to immerse yourself in the Wild West era and preserve a piece of history. Whether you are a fan of Billy the Kid's art, literature, movies, or simply want to own a piece of memorabilia, following these tips will help you on your journey as an aspiring collector.

Chapter 3: Billy, The Kid Historical Tours and Sightseeing

Exploring Billy's Footsteps: Guided Tours of Key Locations

Welcome to the subchapter titled "Exploring Billy's Footsteps: Guided Tours of Key Locations" from the book "Billy, The Kid: A Wild West Legend." In this chapter, we will take you on an exciting journey through the life and adventures of one of the most notorious figures in Wild West history - Billy, The Kid.

For those fascinated by Billy, The Kid, we understand the desire to experience the places where he lived, fought, and left his mark. That's why we have curated a selection of guided tours that will allow you to immerse yourself in his world and gain a deeper understanding of this legendary figure.

Our guided tours will take you to key locations that played a significant role in Billy's life. From his birthplace in New York, where he was born as Henry McCarty, to his early years in New Mexico, where he first began his life of crime, these tours will provide a unique opportunity to walk in Billy's footsteps.

You will have the chance to visit Fort Sumner, the town where Billy met his untimely demise, and explore the infamous Lincoln County War, where Billy's involvement made him a wanted outlaw. Our knowledgeable guides will share intriguing stories, little-known facts, and historical insights, bringing Billy's world to life.

But the adventure doesn't end with the tours. We cater to a wide range of niches related to Billy, The Kid, ensuring that you can find something that piques your interest. Whether you are a collector of Billy, The Kid memorabilia and collectibles, an enthusiast of Wild West art and paintings, a fan of Billy, The Kid novels and literature, or simply someone who enjoys movies and documentaries, there is something for everyone.

Moreover, we offer opportunities to explore Billy, The Kid-themed restaurants, where you can savor delicious food while immersing yourself in the Wild West atmosphere. For those with a penchant for gaming and video games, we have options that allow you to experience the thrill of being Billy, The Kid yourself. And for the music lovers, we have compiled a selection of songs inspired by Billy's adventures.

So, whether you are a history buff, an art lover, a fan of movies and music, or simply curious about this Wild West legend, our guided tours and related experiences will provide an unforgettable journey into the life and times of Billy, The Kid. Join us and discover the allure of the Wild West through the eyes of one of its most iconic figures.

Historic Sites: Museums and Monuments Dedicated to Billy

Billy the Kid, the notorious outlaw and Wild West legend, continues to captivate the imagination of people around the world. His life, filled with daring escapades and a tragic end, has become the stuff of legends. For those who want to delve deeper into the story of this iconic figure, there are numerous museums and monuments dedicated to Billy the Kid, offering a fascinating glimpse into the life and times of this enigmatic character.

One such museum is the Billy the Kid Museum, located in Fort Sumner, New Mexico. This museum houses an impressive collection of memorabilia and artifacts associated with Billy the Kid. Visitors can explore the exhibits, which include original photographs, weapons, clothing, and personal items that once belonged to the outlaw. The museum also provides a comprehensive overview of the events that shaped Billy's life, from his early years to his final days.

Another must-visit destination is the Lincoln Historic Site, located in Lincoln, New Mexico. This site preserves the town where Billy the Kid became a central figure during the infamous Lincoln County War. Visitors can tour the old courthouse where Billy made his daring escape, as well as other historic buildings and landmarks. The site offers guided tours and interactive exhibits that bring the Wild West era to life.

For art enthusiasts, the Billy the Kid Art Gallery in Santa Fe, New Mexico, is a must-see. This gallery features a stunning collection of paintings, sculptures, and other artworks inspired by Billy the Kid. From realistic portraits to abstract interpretations, the artworks on display capture the spirit and mystique of this iconic figure. Visitors can also purchase unique Billy the Kid-inspired art to take home as a memento.

In addition to museums and art galleries, there are also numerous novels, movies, and documentaries dedicated to Billy the Kid. These mediums offer different perspectives on his life and provide further insights into the Wild West era. Fans can immerse themselves in the thrilling tales of his adventures or watch gripping documentaries that shed light on the historical context surrounding his life.

For those who want to truly embrace the Wild West spirit, there are even Billy the Kid themed restaurants and food experiences. These establishments offer a taste of the Old West, with menus featuring hearty cowboy cuisine and drinks inspired by the era. Visitors can enjoy a meal in an authentically decorated setting, complete with memorabilia and photographs of Billy the Kid.

Whether you're a history buff, an art enthusiast, or simply fascinated by the Wild West, exploring the museums, monuments, and other sites dedicated to Billy the Kid is an unforgettable experience. Through these venues, you can gain a deeper understanding of this legendary figure and immerse yourself in the rich history and culture of the Wild West era.

The Wild West Trail: A Journey through Billy's Territory

"The Wild West Trail: A Journey through Billy's Territory"

Welcome to the exciting subchapter titled "The Wild West Trail: A Journey through Billy's Territory" from our book, "Billy, The Kid: A Wild West Legend." In this chapter, we invite you to embark on a thrilling adventure through the untamed lands that once belonged to the notorious outlaw, Billy, The Kid.

For the public who are fascinated by Billy, The Kid, this subchapter offers a chance to delve deeper into his captivating life and the legendary tales that surround him. Discover the man behind the myth, explore his journey, and uncover the truth hidden beneath the layers of history.

Billy, The Kid memorabilia and collectibles enthusiasts will find this subchapter a treasure trove of information. Learn about the rare artifacts and keepsakes associated with this iconic figure. From original wanted posters to vintage weapons, this section will ignite your passion for collecting Billy, The Kid memorabilia.

For those seeking a more immersive experience, we present Billy, The Kid historical tours and sightseeing opportunities. Follow in the footsteps of the outlaw, visiting the places he frequented and the sites where his most infamous events unfolded. Experience the thrill of being transported back in time and immerse yourself in the Wild West era.

Art aficionados will appreciate the section dedicated to Billy, The Kid art and paintings. Discover the various artistic interpretations of this enigmatic figure through stunning visual representations. From classic oil paintings to contemporary mixed media art, this subchapter showcases the diverse range of artistic talent inspired by Billy, The Kid.

Literature enthusiasts will find a collection of Billy, The Kid novels and literature that delves into the intricacies of his life. Explore the pages of gripping biographies, fictional tales, and thought-provoking analysis of this Wild West legend. Immerse yourself in the world of Billy, The Kid through the power of words.

Billy, The Kid movies and documentaries have captivated audiences for decades, and this subchapter presents a curated selection of cinematic works inspired by his life. From Hollywood blockbusters to thought-provoking documentaries, experience the legend of Billy, The Kid through the silver screen.

For those who want to channel their inner outlaw, we offer insights into Billy, The Kid clothing and fashion inspired by the Wild West. Discover the rugged style and timeless fashion that defined the era, and find inspiration for your own Wild West-inspired wardrobe.

Gaming enthusiasts will find a section dedicated to Billy, The Kid gaming and video games. Immerse yourself in interactive adventures that transport you to the Wild West, where you can experience the thrill of being an outlaw or join the pursuit as a lawman.

Photography enthusiasts will appreciate the section on Billy, The Kid photography and vintage photographs. Take a glimpse into the past through breathtaking images that capture the essence of the Wild West and its iconic figures.

No journey through Billy, The Kid's territory would be complete without the accompaniment of music and songs. Explore the melodies that transport you to the heart of the Wild West, where ballads and folk songs immortalize the legends of Billy, The Kid.

Lastly, we invite you to indulge in Billy, The Kid themed restaurants and food experiences. Experience the flavors of the Wild West as you savor dishes inspired by the era. From hearty cowboy meals to creative fusion cuisine, these dining experiences will transport you back in time.

Join us as we embark on "The Wild West Trail: A Journey through Billy's Territory" and discover the captivating legacy of one of history's most famous outlaws, Billy, The Kid. Whether you are a history buff, a collector, an art lover, or simply someone seeking an unforgettable adventure, this subchapter will leave you captivated by the allure of the Wild West.

Unique Experiences: Reenactments and Living History Displays

Immerse yourself in the thrilling world of the Wild West with unique experiences like reenactments and living history displays. Step back in time and witness the legendary escapades of Billy, The Kid, a Wild West icon whose life continues to captivate the imagination of the public.

For avid fans of Billy, The Kid, these reenactments provide an opportunity to witness his daring escapades firsthand. Talented actors don period costumes and recreate key moments from Billy's life, transporting you to a world of outlaws and lawmen. Feel the adrenaline rush as you witness the infamous Lincoln County War unfold before your eyes. These reenactments offer a thrilling and immersive experience, allowing you to feel like you're a part of the action.

In addition to reenactments, living history displays provide a unique way to connect with the past. Step into a recreated Wild West town and interact with costumed interpreters who bring the era to life. From saloons to blacksmith shops, these displays offer an authentic glimpse into the daily lives of the people who lived during Billy's time. Engage in conversations with knowledgeable guides who can answer your questions and provide fascinating insights into the Wild West.

For those with a passion for collecting, these unique experiences offer an opportunity to find rare Billy, The Kid memorabilia and collectibles. Browse through booths filled with vintage photographs, original artwork, and even clothing inspired by the Wild West. Discover treasures that will transport you back in time and allow you to own a piece of Billy, The Kid's legacy.

If you're a fan of literature, movies, or music, these experiences offer a chance to connect with Billy, The Kid through various mediums. Explore Billy, The Kid novels and literature that delve deep into his life and adventures. Watch movies and documentaries that bring his story to the silver screen. Listen to songs that capture the spirit of the Wild West and pay homage to Billy's legendary status. These experiences offer a multi-faceted approach to understanding and appreciating Billy, The Kid's impact on popular culture.

To satisfy your appetite, themed restaurants and food experiences inspired by the Wild West are available. Enjoy a hearty meal in an authentic setting, complete with décor and ambiance that transport you to the era. Indulge in dishes that reflect the flavors of the Wild West, making for a truly immersive and unforgettable dining experience.

Whether you're a history enthusiast, a collector, or simply a fan of the Wild West, reenactments and living history displays offer a unique way to engage with the legend of Billy, The Kid. Step into his world, relive his adventures, and create lasting memories as you immerse yourself in the rich tapestry of the Wild West.

Chapter 4: Billy, The Kid Art and Paintings

Capturing the Outlaw: Famous Artists' Interpretations

In the realm of popular culture, few figures have captured the imagination quite like Billy the Kid. The notorious outlaw, whose exploits and untimely demise have become the stuff of legend, continues to fascinate people from all walks of life. From movies and literature to art and music, Billy the Kid's story has inspired a wide range of creative interpretations.

One of the most enduring forms of artistic expression surrounding Billy the Kid is through paintings and artwork. Renowned artists from different eras have depicted the outlaw in various ways, each offering a unique perspective on his life and legacy. Some artists have chosen to emphasize his rebellious nature, capturing his rugged appearance and fearless demeanor. Others have focused on the romanticized aspects of his story, portraying him as a young, tragic hero of the Wild West. These paintings not only serve as visual representations of Billy the Kid, but also offer a glimpse into the cultural fascination with this enigmatic figure.

Billy the Kid's influence can also be seen in literature, with numerous novels and literary works dedicated to his story. Authors have delved into his complex character, exploring his motivations, relationships, and the circumstances that led to his outlaw lifestyle. These books provide a deeper understanding of the man behind the legend, shedding light on his struggles and the harsh realities of life in the 19th century American West.

In the realm of film and documentaries, Billy the Kid has been portrayed by some of Hollywood's most iconic actors. These cinematic interpretations have brought his story to life, thrilling audiences with tales of gunfights, daring escapes, and the pursuit of justice. Documentaries have also sought to separate fact from fiction, offering a more historically accurate portrayal of Billy the Kid and the events that shaped his life.

For those seeking a tangible connection to Billy the Kid, memorabilia and collectibles offer a way to own a piece of his legend. From vintage photographs and clothing inspired by the Wild West to gaming and video games that immerse players in the outlaw's world, there are countless ways to engage with Billy the Kid's story through physical items.

To truly immerse oneself in the world of Billy the Kid, historical tours and sightseeing experiences are an ideal option. These tours take visitors to the places where he lived, fought, and ultimately met his demise, allowing them to walk in his footsteps and gain a deeper appreciation for the history and culture of the Wild West.

No discussion of Billy the Kid's cultural impact would be complete without mentioning the music and songs inspired by his story. From traditional folk ballads to modern rock anthems, musicians have paid homage to the outlaw through their lyrics and melodies, capturing the essence of his life and times.

Additionally, Billy the Kid-themed restaurants and food experiences provide a unique way to indulge in the Wild West culture. These establishments offer a taste of the era, with menus featuring hearty cowboy fare and decor that transports visitors back to the days of saloons and gunfights.

In conclusion, the artistic interpretations of Billy the Kid have played a significant role in keeping his legend alive. Whether through paintings, literature, film, memorabilia, or music, people from all walks of life can engage with his story and immerse themselves in the rich history and culture of the Wild West. From the public to niche enthusiasts of Billy the Kid and all things related to the Wild West, there is something for everyone to appreciate and enjoy.

The Wild West Aesthetic: Art Inspired by Billy, The Kid

In the realm of Wild West legends, few figures captivate the public's imagination quite like Billy, The Kid. Known for his daring escapades, notorious gunfights, and enigmatic persona, Billy, The Kid has become an icon of the American frontier. This subchapter explores the artistic expressions that have emerged from the mystique surrounding this legendary outlaw.

Artists from various genres and mediums have drawn inspiration from Billy, The Kid's adventurous life and the spirit of the Wild West. Painters have captured his rugged charm, often depicting him astride a horse, his trusty six-shooter at the ready. These artworks transport viewers back to the untamed landscapes of the American frontier, evoking a sense of danger and excitement that defined Billy, The Kid's era.

Literature has also embraced Billy, The Kid as a compelling protagonist. Novels and biographies offer readers an opportunity to delve deeper into his complex character, exploring the motivations behind his actions and the legacy he left behind. These literary works transport us to a time when lawlessness reigned supreme, and the line between hero and villain blurred.

Movies and documentaries have played a significant role in immortalizing Billy, The Kid's story on the silver screen. From early black-and-white films to modern adaptations, audiences have been captivated by the drama, romance, and tragedy of his life. These cinematic interpretations bring the Wild West to life, showcasing the gritty realities and larger-than-life characters that defined this era.

The Wild West aesthetic has also influenced fashion and clothing. Inspired by the rugged charm of Billy, The Kid and his contemporaries, designers have incorporated elements of Western attire into their collections. From cowboy boots and Stetson hats to fringed jackets and denim, these fashion trends pay homage to the timeless allure of the Wild West.

For those seeking a taste of history, Billy, The Kid historical tours and sightseeing offer a chance to walk in the footsteps of the legendary outlaw. These immersive experiences allow visitors to explore the landscapes where Billy, The Kid roamed, visiting landmarks and hearing tales of his daring escapades.

Billy, The Kid's influence extends beyond the realms of art, literature, and fashion. Music has also paid homage to this Wild West legend, with songs and ballads recounting his exploits and immortalizing his name. Additionally, photography and vintage photographs provide a glimpse into the past, capturing the spirit of the American frontier and preserving the memory of Billy, The Kid for generations to come.

In the realm of entertainment, gaming and video games have allowed enthusiasts to step into the boots of Billy, The Kid, experiencing the adrenaline-fueled adventures of the Wild West firsthand. These interactive experiences transport players to a time when outlaws ruled the land, offering a thrilling escape into the past.

Lastly, for those craving a culinary adventure, Billy, The Kid themed restaurants and food experiences serve up a taste of the Wild West. From hearty dishes inspired by cowboy campfire cooking to saloons that transport patrons back to the era of Billy, The Kid, these establishments offer a unique dining experience steeped in history and nostalgia.

Billy, The Kid's legacy continues to captivate and inspire the public. Whether through art, literature, fashion, or entertainment, his influence on popular culture remains as enduring as the American frontier itself. Explore the Wild West aesthetic inspired by Billy, The Kid and immerse yourself in the timeless allure of the American frontier.

Creating Your Own Masterpiece: Tips for Western Art

Introduction:

In the world of Western art, the legend of Billy the Kid has captivated the imaginations of artists across various mediums. From paintings to novels, movies to music, his story continues to inspire countless works of art. Whether you are an established artist or simply someone who appreciates Western art, this subchapter offers tips and guidance for creating your own masterpiece inspired by the Wild West and the iconic figure of Billy the Kid.

1. Immerse Yourself in Billy the Kid's Story:

Before creating your artwork, immerse yourself in the fascinating story of Billy the Kid. Read books, watch documentaries, and visit historical sites to gain a deeper understanding of his life and the Wild West era. This knowledge will bring authenticity and depth to your artwork.

2. Choose Your Medium:

Decide on the medium that best suits your artistic style and vision. Western art can be expressed through various mediums, such as painting, photography, music, or even fashion. Choose the medium that resonates with you and allows you to express your creativity effectively.

3. Capture the Spirit of the Wild West:

When creating your masterpiece, focus on capturing the essence and spirit of the Wild West. Incorporate elements such as rugged landscapes, cowboys, horses, and the iconic imagery associated with Billy the Kid.

Use colors, textures, and techniques that evoke the rawness and vitality of the era.

4. Pay Attention to Detail:

To create a truly remarkable piece of Western art, pay attention to the details. Study historical photographs, clothing, and artifacts from the time period to ensure accuracy and authenticity in your artwork. Attention to detail will enhance the overall impact of your masterpiece.

5. Experiment and Innovate:

While staying true to the Western art genre, don't be afraid to experiment and innovate. Infuse your own unique style and perspective into your artwork, allowing it to stand out among others. Be bold, take risks, and let your creativity shine.

6. Share Your Artwork:

Once your masterpiece is complete, share it with the world. Display your artwork in galleries, participate in art shows, or create an online portfolio to reach a wider audience. Engage with the Billy the Kid community and art enthusiasts to gain feedback and recognition for your work.

Conclusion:

Creating your own masterpiece inspired by Billy the Kid and the Wild West is a rewarding and exhilarating experience. By immersing yourself in the story, choosing the right medium, capturing the spirit of the Wild West, paying attention to detail, and incorporating your own unique style, you can create a truly remarkable piece of Western art. Share your artwork with the world and join the vibrant community of Billy the Kid enthusiasts who continue to celebrate and honor the legacy of this Wild West legend.

Chapter 5: Billy, The Kid Novels and Literature

Billy, The Kid in Fiction: Popular Novels and Series

Billy, The Kid, the legendary outlaw of the Wild West, has captivated the imaginations of people for generations. His story, filled with daring escapades, gunfights, and a tragic end, has inspired numerous works of fiction in various forms of media. From novels and series to movies, documentaries, and even video games, Billy, The Kid's legacy lives on through the creative interpretations of talented storytellers.

In the realm of literature, Billy, The Kid has become a beloved character in popular novels and series. Authors have delved into his life, painting vivid portraits of his adventures, struggles, and the myth surrounding him. These novels offer readers a chance to immerse themselves in the gritty world of the Wild West and experience the thrill of Billy, The Kid's exploits firsthand.

For fans of Billy, The Kid, these novels offer a unique opportunity to delve deeper into his character and understand the complexities of his life. They breathe life into the legend, providing a glimpse into the man behind the myth. Whether you're a history buff or simply fascinated by tales of outlaws and cowboys, these novels are sure to captivate and entertain.

Alongside the novels, Billy, The Kid's story has also made its way onto the silver screen. Countless movies and documentaries have been made, showcasing different perspectives on his life and the events that shaped him. These visual adaptations bring Billy, The Kid's story to life, allowing audiences to witness the action-packed events and the iconic moments that have made him a cultural icon.

Beyond literature and film, Billy, The Kid's influence extends to other realms of creativity. His image has been immortalized in paintings, photographs, and even fashion inspired by the Wild West. Art lovers can find stunning depictions of Billy, The Kid, capturing his rebellious spirit and the rugged landscapes of his time. Collectors of memorabilia can also find a plethora of items, from vintage photographs to clothing and accessories that pay homage to the legend.

For those seeking a truly immersive experience, Billy, The Kid historical tours and sightseeing offer a chance to walk in his footsteps. These tours take visitors to the places where Billy, The Kid lived, fought, and met his tragic end. As you explore the towns and landscapes of the Wild West, you can imagine the thrill and danger that Billy, The Kid faced on a daily basis.

Billy, The Kid's influence can also be found in music, with songs that tell his tales of adventure and tragedy. These songs capture the essence of the Wild West and evoke the spirit of this notorious outlaw. Additionally, themed restaurants and food experiences allow fans to indulge in the flavors of the era, transporting them back to the time when Billy, The Kid roamed the frontier.

Finally, for those looking for interactive entertainment, Billy, The Kid gaming and video games provide an immersive experience. Whether you're playing as the legendary outlaw or exploring the Wild West in virtual reality, these games offer a chance to step into Billy, The Kid's boots and experience the thrill of the frontier.

In conclusion, Billy, The Kid's legacy continues to thrive through popular novels and series, movies and documentaries, art and paintings, clothing and fashion, gaming and video games, photography and vintage photographs, music and songs, themed restaurants, and historical tours. This wide range of creative expressions ensures that Billy, The Kid's captivating story will continue to captivate and inspire audiences for years to come.

Historical Accounts: Non-Fiction Books about Billy

Billy, The Kid: A Wild West Legend is not only a thrilling tale of the infamous outlaw's life but also a comprehensive guide to the myriad of ways in which Billy's legacy has been immortalized throughout history. In this subchapter, we delve into the world of non-fiction books that provide a deep insight into the life and times of Billy, The Kid.

For those seeking an in-depth understanding of Billy's exploits, there is a plethora of non-fiction books available. These meticulously researched accounts shed light on the true events that shaped Billy's life, separating fact from fiction. From biographies written by historians to firsthand accounts from individuals who crossed paths with the legendary outlaw, these books offer a captivating glimpse into the Wild West.

The popularity of Billy, The Kid transcends the pages of literature and has inspired various industries. Billy, The Kid memorabilia and collectibles have become highly sought after by enthusiasts and collectors alike. From vintage photographs and authentic artifacts to replicas of Billy's iconic revolver, these items allow fans to own a piece of history.

For those eager to immerse themselves in Billy's world, historical tours and sightseeing opportunities are available. These guided experiences take you through the very places where Billy roamed, providing a unique perspective on his life and the Wild West era. Additionally, art enthusiasts can explore the realm of Billy, The Kid art and paintings, where talented artists capture his spirit and the rugged landscapes of the time.

The impact of Billy, The Kid extends to the realms of literature, movies, and documentaries. Countless novels and literary works have been penned, offering fictionalized accounts of Billy's escapades. Meanwhile, movies and documentaries bring his story to life on the silver screen, allowing audiences to witness the untamed adventures of this Wild West legend.

Beyond the realms of entertainment, the influence of Billy, The Kid can be seen in fashion, gaming, photography, music, and even culinary experiences. Inspired by the rugged charm of the Wild West, clothing lines and fashion collections pay homage to Billy's iconic style. Gaming enthusiasts can enjoy video games that recreate the thrilling atmosphere of the era, while vintage photographs and photography exhibitions capture the essence of the time. Billy's legend is even celebrated through themed restaurants and food experiences, offering patrons a taste of the Wild West through their menus and ambiance.

In conclusion, the historical accounts of Billy, The Kid found in non-fiction books provide a fascinating glimpse into his life and legacy. From literature to visual arts, movies to music, and even fashion to culinary experiences, the influence of Billy, The Kid can be felt in a multitude of ways. Whether you're a history buff, a collector, or simply intrigued by the Wild West, these non-fiction books are a must-read for any fan of this legendary outlaw.

Unraveling the Myth: Biographies and Scholarly Works

In the realm of Billy, The Kid, the notorious Wild West legend, the public has been captivated by the enigmatic persona and thrilling tales surrounding his life. Countless books, articles, and scholarly works have been written to shed light on the truth behind the myth. These works not only serve as windows into the past but also cater to the diverse interests of the Billy, The Kid enthusiasts, spanning from memorabilia collectors to history buffs, art enthusiasts, literature lovers, and even gamers.

Biographies dedicated to Billy, The Kid provide an in-depth exploration of his life, from his humble beginnings to his infamous outlaw days. These books meticulously piece together historical records, eyewitness accounts, and archival materials to present a comprehensive and accurate portrait of the man behind the myth. For those seeking to delve deeper into the true story, these biographies offer a fascinating journey through the Wild West.

Beyond biographies, scholarly works examine Billy, The Kid's impact on American history and culture. These works delve into the social and political context of the time, shedding light on the factors that shaped his life and the legends that arose from it. They provide a critical analysis of the various narratives surrounding Billy, The Kid, challenging popular misconceptions and offering new perspectives.

For those who wish to immerse themselves in the world of Billy, The Kid, there is a wide range of mediums to explore. Art enthusiasts can indulge in paintings and artworks inspired by the Wild West, capturing the essence of Billy, The Kid's era. Historical tours and sightseeing options take visitors back in time, allowing them to walk in the footsteps of the legendary outlaw.

Literature lovers can enjoy novels and literature that bring Billy, The Kid's story to life, while movies and documentaries offer visual interpretations of his adventures. Vintage photographs and photography exhibitions provide glimpses into the past, offering a tangible connection to the Wild West.

Billy, The Kid's influence extends beyond traditional mediums, reaching into the realms of clothing, fashion, and even gaming. Fashion enthusiasts can embrace the Wild West aesthetic through clothing inspired by Billy, The Kid and his era. Gamers can immerse themselves in virtual worlds that recreate the Wild West, allowing them to experience the thrill of being an outlaw.

For those seeking a multisensory experience, themed restaurants and food experiences transport diners to the Wild West, tantalizing their taste buds with dishes inspired by the era. Music and songs set the tone, evoking the spirit of Billy, The Kid and the Wild West, creating an immersive atmosphere.

In conclusion, the world of Billy, The Kid is a rich tapestry, interwoven with biographies, scholarly works, art, literature, movies, photography, music, and even culinary experiences. Whether you are a collector, a history enthusiast, an art lover, or simply curious about the Wild West, these resources offer a gateway to unraveling the myth and discovering the true story of this legendary figure.

Chapter 6: Billy, The Kid Movies and Documentaries

Hollywood's Take: Iconic Films Featuring Billy, The Kid

Billy, The Kid: A Wild West Legend invites you to dive into the captivating world of one of the most notorious figures in American history. In this subchapter, we explore the influence of Hollywood on the enduring legacy of Billy, The Kid. From films that sparked imaginations to the creation of memorabilia and collectibles, Billy, The Kid's story has left an indelible mark on popular culture.

For decades, Billy, The Kid has fascinated filmmakers, leading to the creation of iconic movies and documentaries. These cinematic interpretations have allowed audiences to experience the thrilling adventures and complex character of this Wild West legend. From the early days of the silver screen to modern blockbusters, Billy, The Kid has been portrayed by legendary actors such as Paul Newman, Emilio Estevez, and Kris Kristofferson.

The impact of Billy, The Kid's story extends beyond movies. It has inspired a plethora of art and paintings that capture the essence of the Wild West. Renowned artists have depicted Billy, The Kid's daring escapades and enigmatic persona, making these artworks highly sought after by collectors and enthusiasts alike.

Fans of Billy, The Kid can also embark on historical tours and sightseeing adventures to explore the places where this legendary outlaw once roamed. Immerse yourself in the landscapes that shaped his life, reliving the stories that have been passed down through generations.

The allure of Billy, The Kid extends to literature as well, with numerous novels and literature dedicated to his exploits. These works offer unique perspectives and delve into the complexities of this Wild West figure, allowing readers to dive deeper into his character and the tumultuous times he lived in.

If you're looking to embrace the spirit of Billy, The Kid, you'll find a wide range of clothing and fashion inspired by the Wild West. Whether it's cowboy hats, boots, or rugged denim jackets, you can channel your inner outlaw with style.

For gaming enthusiasts, there are even video games that allow you to step into the shoes of Billy, The Kid, experiencing his adventures firsthand. Immerse yourself in the Wild West and test your skills in a world filled with danger and excitement.

To capture the essence of the era, explore the world of Billy, The Kid through vintage photographs and photography. These glimpses into the past offer a captivating window into the life and times of this Wild West legend.

Music has also been deeply influenced by Billy, The Kid. From folk songs to country ballads, musicians have crafted melodies and lyrics that tell his story, evoking the spirit of the Wild West and the legend that still captivates us today.

To truly immerse yourself in the world of Billy, The Kid, you can even visit themed restaurants and indulge in food experiences reminiscent of the Wild West. From hearty cowboy fare to creative cocktails, these establishments offer a unique dining experience that transports you back in time.

In conclusion, Hollywood has played a significant role in shaping the enduring fascination with Billy, The Kid. From movies to literature, art, and music, his legend continues to captivate the imagination of the public. Whether you're a fan of collectibles, historical tours, or simply want to experience the thrill of the Wild West, there is something for everyone in the world of Billy, The Kid.

True Crime Documentaries: Examining Billy's Story

In the world of true crime, few figures capture the imagination quite like Billy the Kid. Known as a Wild West legend, Billy's story has fascinated people for generations, inspiring everything from movies and novels to collectibles and historical tours. But who was the real Billy the Kid, and what do we truly know about his life and crimes?

This subchapter delves into the realm of true crime documentaries, offering a closer look at Billy's story and the various ways it has been portrayed on screen. Whether you're a die-hard fan of Billy the Kid or simply curious about the Wild West era, this exploration is sure to captivate and educate.

Billy's story is one that has been shrouded in myth and legend, making it a perfect subject for true crime documentaries. These films aim to separate fact from fiction, shedding light on the true events that shaped Billy's life and his role in the lawless frontier. By examining historical records, eyewitness accounts, and expert analysis, these documentaries offer a comprehensive and objective perspective on Billy's story.

For the public, true crime documentaries provide a unique opportunity to step into the shoes of the infamous outlaw. Through expert interviews, archival footage, and dramatic reenactments, viewers can immerse themselves in the world of Billy the Kid. These documentaries not only entertain but also educate, revealing the complexities of Billy's character and the historical context in which he lived.

For those passionate about Billy the Kid, these documentaries offer a chance to further explore their interests. From memorabilia and collectibles to art and paintings inspired by the Wild West, fans can deepen their connection to Billy's story through various mediums.

Additionally, historical tours and sightseeing trips allow enthusiasts to walk in the footsteps of the legendary outlaw, visiting the locations where key events unfolded.

The impact of Billy the Kid extends beyond documentaries and collectibles. His story has inspired clothing and fashion trends, with Western-style attire enjoying a resurgence in popularity. Gaming and video games have also taken inspiration from the Wild West, allowing players to experience the thrill and danger of life as an outlaw. And let's not forget the power of music, with songs and compositions celebrating Billy's exploits.

In conclusion, true crime documentaries provide a captivating and informative lens through which to examine Billy the Kid's story. They offer the public a chance to explore the truth behind the legend, while also catering to the diverse interests of Billy the Kid enthusiasts. From novels and movies to clothing and gaming, Billy's legacy continues to captivate audiences across multiple niches, ensuring his place as one of the most enduring figures in Wild West history.

The Director's Perspective: Behind-the-Scenes of Billy, The Kid Films

Welcome to a behind-the-scenes look at the making of the iconic Billy, The Kid films. As the director of these movies, I have had the privilege of bringing this legendary Wild West character to life on the big screen. In this subchapter, I will share some fascinating insights into the creative process, challenges faced, and the impact of Billy, The Kid films on popular culture.

When it comes to portraying such a notorious figure like Billy, The Kid, attention to historical accuracy is crucial. As the director, I worked closely with historians and experts to capture the essence of the time period, ensuring the costumes, sets, and locations were authentic. This attention to detail not only adds credibility to the films but also appeals to the niche of Billy, The Kid memorabilia and collectibles. Fans of the Wild West era can now own a piece of history through these meticulously crafted props and costumes.

The popularity of Billy, The Kid films has also led to an increased interest in historical tours and sightseeing. Fans can now visit the actual locations where Billy, The Kid roamed, providing a unique opportunity to immerse themselves in the legend's footsteps. For those who appreciate art and paintings, the landscapes showcased in the films have inspired a new wave of artists, capturing the spirit of the Wild West in their artwork.

Moreover, Billy, The Kid novels and literature have experienced a resurgence, with authors drawing inspiration from the films to create gripping tales of adventure and rebellion. The movies have also spawned a collection of documentaries, delving deeper into the life and times of Billy, The Kid, catering to the audience's thirst for knowledge.

The influence of the Billy, The Kid films extends beyond the world of cinema. It has inspired a fashion trend, with clothing and accessories inspired by the Wild West becoming increasingly popular. Additionally, gaming enthusiasts can now experience the thrill of the Wild West through video games that transport players into the boots of Billy, The Kid.

Photography and vintage photographs of Billy, The Kid have become highly sought after, as fans seek to capture a glimpse of this legendary outlaw. The films' soundtracks have also resonated with audiences, with Billy, The Kid songs becoming anthems of the Wild West.

Lastly, Billy, The Kid-themed restaurants and food experiences have emerged, allowing fans to indulge in a culinary journey through the Wild West. From hearty cowboy meals to themed cocktails, these establishments offer a unique dining experience.

In conclusion, the impact of Billy, The Kid films reaches far beyond the cinema screen. From collectibles to literature, fashion to gaming, this Wild West legend continues to captivate the public's imagination, leaving an indelible mark on popular culture.

Chapter 7: Billy, The Kid Clothing and Fashion Inspired by the Wild West

Western Chic: Incorporating Billy's Style into Modern Fashion

Billy the Kid, a notorious Wild West legend, continues to captivate the public's imagination with his daring escapades and rugged charm. His iconic style, a fusion of rugged cowboy and rebellious outlaw, has become a timeless fashion inspiration. In this subchapter, we explore how you can incorporate Billy's style into modern fashion, allowing you to channel the spirit of the Wild West in a chic and contemporary way.

One of the key elements of Billy's style is his signature cowboy hat. Embrace this classic accessory by opting for a wide-brimmed hat in a neutral color, such as brown or black. Pair it with a tailored blazer, a crisp white shirt, and a pair of well-fitted jeans for a modern take on the cowboy look. Complete the ensemble with a pair of worn-in leather boots, reminiscent of Billy's rugged lifestyle.

Another way to incorporate Billy's style into your wardrobe is through the use of fringe. Fringed jackets, skirts, or accessories add a touch of Western flair to any outfit. Opt for a suede fringe jacket paired with a simple t-shirt and skinny jeans for a contemporary twist on this classic look. For a more subtle approach, accessorize with a fringed bag or a statement belt.

Billy's style also embraced denim, a fabric synonymous with the Wild West. Experiment with denim on denim looks by pairing a chambray shirt with distressed jeans, or try a denim jacket over a floral dress for a juxtaposition of feminine and rugged elements.

Accessories play a crucial role in completing the Western chic look. Consider adding a statement belt with a large buckle or a vintage-inspired bandana tied around your neck. These small touches can instantly elevate your outfit and pay homage to Billy's iconic style.

In conclusion, incorporating Billy's style into modern fashion allows you to embrace the spirit of the Wild West while maintaining a contemporary aesthetic. By incorporating elements such as cowboy hats, fringe, denim, and statement accessories, you can channel Billy's rebellious charm in a chic and fashionable way. Whether you're attending a Western-themed event, exploring the Wild West on a historical tour, or simply looking to express your love for Billy the Kid, these fashion tips will help you create a Western chic look that is both timeless and on-trend.

The Cowboy Look: Historical Clothing and Accessories

In the wild and rugged era of the Wild West, one figure stands out as the epitome of the cowboy spirit - Billy, The Kid. This subchapter explores the iconic clothing and accessories that defined the Cowboy Look, a style that continues to captivate the public's imagination to this day. From clothing and memorabilia to tours and themed restaurants, the influence of Billy, The Kid and the Wild West can be seen in various niches.

When it comes to Billy, The Kid memorabilia and collectibles, one cannot overlook the significance of historical clothing and accessories. From the classic wide-brimmed hat to the leather boots, these items were not just fashion statements but practical gear for the rugged lifestyle of the cowboys. Many collectors seek out authentic pieces from the era or replicas that exude the spirit of the Wild West.

For enthusiasts looking to immerse themselves in the world of Billy, The Kid, historical tours and sightseeing offer a chance to step back in time. These tours often include visits to key locations associated with Billy, The

Kid, allowing participants to envision the clothing and accessories worn by the legendary figure and his contemporaries.

Artists and painters have also found inspiration in the Cowboy Look and Billy, The Kid's iconic image. Through their works, they capture the essence of the Wild West, often depicting cowboys wearing traditional attire and accessories. These paintings serve as a visual reminder of the enduring appeal of the Cowboy Look.

Literature and film have played a significant role in shaping our perception of Billy, The Kid and the Wild West. Novels, movies, and documentaries often feature characters dressed in cowboy clothing, evoking a sense of adventure and rugged individualism. These portrayals have further fueled the public's fascination with the Cowboy Look.

The Cowboy Look has also made its mark in the fashion industry, inspiring clothing lines and accessories that pay homage to the Wild West. From fringe jackets to bolo ties, modern interpretations of cowboy fashion can be seen on runways and in everyday attire. The Cowboy Look has become a timeless style that continues to influence contemporary fashion.

The influence of Billy, The Kid's era extends beyond clothing and fashion. The Wild West has become a popular theme in gaming and video games, with players immersing themselves in virtual cowboy adventures. Additionally, vintage photographs, music, and songs evoke a sense of nostalgia for this bygone era, captivating both enthusiasts and the general public.

Finally, the fascination with Billy, The Kid and the Wild West extends to themed restaurants and food experiences. These establishments often embrace the Cowboy Look in their decor, offering patrons a taste of the rugged lifestyle through hearty meals and Western-inspired ambiance.

In conclusion, the Cowboy Look, with its historical clothing and accessories, continues to captivate the public's imagination across various niches. From memorabilia and collectibles to tours, literature, film, fashion, gaming, photography, music, and even themed restaurants, the influence of Billy, The Kid and the Wild West is evident. Whether you're a fan of Billy, The Kid or simply drawn to the rugged charm of the Cowboy Look, there are numerous avenues to explore and immerse yourself in this iconic style.

Wild West Fashion Icons: Influential Figures in Western Style

Western fashion has always been synonymous with the Wild West, evoking images of rugged cowboys, outlaws, and lawmen. In this subchapter, we explore the influential figures who shaped the iconic style of the Wild West and continue to inspire fashion trends today.

One of the most notorious figures in Wild West history is Billy the Kid. Known for his daring escapades and rebellious spirit, Billy the Kid became an unexpected fashion icon of his time. Despite his short life, his unique sense of style left a lasting impact on the fashion industry and continues to captivate the public's imagination.

Billy the Kid's signature look included a wide-brimmed hat, a fringed leather jacket, and a pair of well-worn cowboy boots. These iconic pieces became synonymous with the Wild West and have been replicated in countless movies, fashion collections, and memorabilia.

The influence of Wild West fashion extends far beyond Billy the Kid. Other influential figures in Western style include famous lawmen like Wyatt Earp and Wild Bill Hickok, whose tailored suits and elegant accessories brought a touch of sophistication to the dusty streets of the frontier.

Artists and photographers also played a vital role in shaping the Wild West fashion aesthetic. The work of renowned photographer William

Henry Jackson captured the ruggedness and romance of the West, showcasing cowboys in their distinctive attire. These images not only immortalized the fashion of the era but also contributed to the rise of Western-themed fashion in the years to come.

Today, the influence of Wild West fashion can be seen in various niches. Collectors of Billy the Kid memorabilia and enthusiasts of Western-themed art and literature seek out items that pay homage to this iconic era. Historical tours and sightseeing experiences offer an opportunity to step back in time and explore the fashion of the Wild West firsthand.

The Wild West has also inspired clothing lines, with designers incorporating elements such as fringe, denim, and leather into their collections. From high fashion runways to everyday street style, the Western aesthetic continues to make a statement.

In conclusion, Wild West fashion icons like Billy the Kid have left an indelible mark on the fashion world. Their unique style, rugged yet refined, continues to inspire and captivate audiences across various niches. Whether it's through collectibles, tours, art, literature, movies, or clothing, the Wild West fashion remains a timeless symbol of adventure, rebellion, and individuality.

Chapter 8: Billy, The Kid Gaming and Video Games

Digital Adventures: Popular Video Games with Billy, The Kid Themes

In the modern era of technology and gaming, the Wild West legend of Billy, The Kid has found a new platform to captivate audiences - video games. This subchapter explores the exciting world of digital adventures that pay homage to the infamous outlaw and his thrilling escapades.

For gaming enthusiasts and fans of Billy, The Kid, these video games offer an immersive experience that allows players to step into the shoes of the legendary gunslinger. From intense shootouts in dusty towns to daring horseback chases through rugged landscapes, these games transport players back to the lawless days of the Wild West.

One popular video game title that features Billy, The Kid themes is "Outlaw Redemption." In this game, players embark on a quest for justice as they navigate through a vast open-world environment inspired by the landscapes of New Mexico. With stunning graphics and realistic gameplay mechanics, players can engage in thrilling gunfights, engage in high-stakes poker games, and even experience the adrenaline rush of robbing trains.

For those seeking a more strategic and immersive gaming experience, "Billy's Legacy" offers a unique blend of action and storytelling. Set in the late 1800s, players must make critical decisions that shape Billy's fate as they navigate through a branching narrative filled with moral dilemmas and unexpected twists. With stunning visuals and a captivating storyline, this game allows players to truly immerse themselves in the life and times of Billy, The Kid.

In addition to these action-packed games, fans of Billy, The Kid can also explore virtual museums and historical recreations in games such as "Billy's Frontier." This game offers players an opportunity to wander through meticulously recreated towns and landmarks from the Wild West era, complete with historical artifacts and interactive exhibits.

Whether you are a gamer, history enthusiast, or simply a fan of Billy, The Kid, these video games provide a thrilling and educational experience. Immerse yourself in the Wild West, test your skills as an outlaw, and embark on exciting adventures with Billy, The Kid as your guide. Let the digital world bring the legend to life like never before.

Interactive Experiences: Virtual Reality and Augmented Reality Games

In the fast-paced world of technology, virtual reality (VR) and augmented reality (AR) have revolutionized the way we experience entertainment. From gaming to history, these immersive mediums have found their way into the realm of Billy the Kid, offering fans and enthusiasts unique and engaging experiences like never before.

For Billy the Kid fans, VR and AR games have opened up a whole new dimension to explore and interact with the Wild West legend. Imagine stepping into the shoes of this notorious outlaw, wandering through the dusty streets of old Western towns, engaging in thrilling shootouts, and experiencing the adrenaline rush of a life on the run. With VR headsets, players can immerse themselves in a virtual world, where they become part of Billy the Kid's enthralling story.

These interactive experiences not only provide an escape into a bygone era but also offer a chance to learn more about Billy the Kid's historical significance. Through meticulously designed virtual environments, players can visit iconic landmarks, such as the Lincoln County Courthouse or Fort Sumner, and engage with historically accurate characters who bring Billy's legend to life. The combination of detailed storytelling and cutting-edge technology creates an educational and entertaining experience for both history enthusiasts and fans of Billy the Kid.

Moreover, these interactive experiences extend beyond gaming. Virtual reality offers the opportunity to explore Billy the Kid memorabilia and collectibles in a digital museum-like setting. Through VR, fans can examine rare artifacts, read historical documents, and even own virtual versions of items associated with Billy the Kid. This not only enhances the accessibility of such collectibles but also allows individuals to experience a piece of history firsthand.

In addition to gaming and collectibles, virtual reality and augmented reality have influenced other niches related to Billy the Kid. From art and paintings inspired by the Wild West to novels and literature centered around his life, these technologies offer a new way to enjoy and engage with these mediums. Furthermore, VR and AR can transport individuals to Billy the Kid-themed restaurants, where they can savor the flavors of the Wild West while being immersed in a virtual environment reminiscent of the time.

As technology continues to advance, the possibilities for interactive experiences related to Billy the Kid are endless. Whether it's through gaming, collectibles, art, or even dining, virtual reality and augmented reality provide an exciting avenue for fans to delve deeper into the legend of Billy the Kid and the rich history of the Wild West.

Becoming an Outlaw: Role-Playing Games set in the Wild West

Immerse yourself in the thrilling world of the Wild West with role-playing games set in this iconic era. Step into the boots of legendary outlaws like Billy the Kid and experience the adrenaline rush of life on the frontier. In this subchapter, we explore how these games allow you to become an outlaw, shaping your own destiny in the untamed West.

For fans of Billy the Kid, these role-playing games offer a unique opportunity to delve into his notorious life. Experience the thrill of his daring escapades, from his early days as a cattle rustler to his later exploits as a feared gunslinger. With detailed historical accuracy, you can relive the excitement of Billy's adventures, encountering famous figures and exploring iconic locations.

As you navigate the game's immersive landscapes, you'll encounter a vast array of challenges and choices. Will you join a gang of outlaws, robbing banks and trains, or will you carve your own path as a solitary gunslinger? The decisions you make will shape your character's reputation and the world around you.

The Wild West backdrop provides the perfect canvas for thrilling gameplay. Engage in intense shootouts, engage in high-stakes poker games, and experience the harsh realities of survival in this lawless land. With stunning graphics and authentic soundtracks, these games transport you to a time when the West was truly wild.

Beyond the exhilarating gameplay, role-playing games set in the Wild West offer a range of other immersive experiences. From Billy the Kid memorabilia and collectibles to historical tours and sightseeing, there are endless ways to further indulge in this captivating era. Dive into Billy the Kid art and paintings, explore novels and literature inspired by his life, or lose yourself in movies and documentaries that bring his legend to life.

For those with a passion for fashion, you can even find Wild West-inspired clothing and accessories, allowing you to embody the rugged style of the outlaws. Capture the essence of the era with vintage photographs and photography, or embrace the music and songs that defined the Wild West.

If you're looking to satisfy your taste buds, why not try Billy the Kid-themed restaurants and food experiences? Indulge in hearty Western cuisine while immersing yourself in the atmosphere of the era.

For avid gamers, the Wild West provides an exciting backdrop for immersive adventures. Whether you're a fan of Billy the Kid or simply drawn to the allure of the frontier, these role-playing games offer a unique opportunity to become an outlaw and experience the thrill of the Wild West firsthand.

Chapter 9: Billy, The Kid Photography and Vintage Photographs

Preserving History: Collecting and Restoring Billy, The Kid Photos

In the realm of the Wild West, one name stands out among the rest - Billy, The Kid. As a legendary figure of the American frontier, his story has captivated the public for decades. From movies and documentaries to novels and songs, Billy, The Kid's legacy lives on in various forms of art and entertainment. However, one aspect that truly preserves the essence of this iconic figure is the collection and restoration of his vintage photographs.

Billy, The Kid memorabilia and collectibles enthusiasts understand the significance of owning a piece of history. These rare vintage photographs not only offer a glimpse into the life and times of Billy, The Kid, but they also provide a tangible connection to the Wild West era. By carefully collecting and preserving these photographs, we ensure that future generations can appreciate and learn from the past.

For those who seek a more immersive experience, Billy, The Kid historical tours and sightseeing opportunities are a must. Imagine walking in the footsteps of the infamous outlaw, exploring the places he roamed and the landscapes that shaped his story. These tours often feature stops at museums and exhibits that showcase original and restored Billy, The Kid photographs, allowing visitors to witness the past come alive before their eyes.

Art enthusiasts, too, can find inspiration in Billy, The Kid's story. Artists have long been fascinated by the Wild West, and many have immortalized Billy, The Kid through their paintings and sculptures. By studying vintage photographs, artists can capture the essence of this enigmatic figure, bringing his spirit to life on canvas or in clay.

Moreover, the influence of Billy, The Kid extends beyond traditional art forms. The fashion industry has embraced the rugged charm of the Wild West, creating clothing and accessories inspired by the era. From cowboy boots to fringe jackets, these fashion pieces allow individuals to channel their inner outlaw and pay homage to Billy, The Kid's legacy.

Even the world of gaming and video games has been touched by Billy, The Kid's story. Developers have created interactive experiences that allow players to immerse themselves in the Wild West, taking on the role of outlaws or lawmen in virtual landscapes reminiscent of Billy, The Kid's adventures.

In conclusion, the collection and restoration of Billy, The Kid photographs play a vital role in preserving history and ensuring that his story continues to captivate the public. Whether it's through memorabilia, historical tours, art, fashion, gaming, or other mediums, Billy, The Kid's legacy lives on, allowing us to connect with the spirit of the Wild West and experience the thrill of an era long gone.

Capturing the Essence: Modern Photography Inspired by Billy

In the realm of modern photography, no figure has captivated the imagination quite like Billy the Kid. His enigmatic persona, rugged charm, and wild exploits have made him an enduring icon of the Wild West. Today, photographers from all walks of life are inspired by Billy's legend, seeking to capture his essence through their lenses.

This subchapter explores the world of modern photography, paying homage to Billy the Kid and the impact he has had on various artistic mediums. Whether you're a fan of Billy's outlaw persona, a history buff, or simply appreciate the art of photography, this section will pique your interest.

Many skilled photographers have taken up the challenge of immortalizing Billy's spirit through their work. From capturing the vast landscapes that Billy roamed to recreating iconic moments from his life, these artists use their lenses to bring his legend to life.

Some photographers focus on the vintage aesthetic, using techniques and equipment reminiscent of the era in which Billy lived. Their work transports viewers back in time, offering a glimpse into the rough and tumble world of the Wild West.

Others take a more contemporary approach, blending the past and present to create visually striking images that evoke a sense of nostalgia. These photographers often experiment with color, light, and composition to convey the essence of Billy's story in a unique and thought-provoking way.

Photography inspired by Billy the Kid has found its way into various artistic mediums. From paintings and novels to movies and documentaries, his story continues to resonate with artists worldwide. His image adorns clothing and fashion inspired by the Wild West, and his legend even finds a place in the world of gaming and video games.

For those seeking a deeper connection to Billy's world, historical tours and sightseeing expeditions offer a chance to walk in his footsteps. These tours often include visits to the very locations where Billy roamed, providing a tangible connection to his story.

Billy the Kid's influence extends beyond the visual arts. His legend has inspired musicians to write songs and compose music that captures the spirit of the Wild West. And for those looking to immerse themselves fully in the experience, themed restaurants and food experiences offer a taste of the Wild West, complete with hearty meals and a vibrant atmosphere.

Whether you're a collector of Billy the Kid memorabilia and collectibles or simply curious about his story, the world of modern photography offers a window into his captivating world. Through the lens of talented photographers, Billy's essence comes to life, ensuring that his legend continues to inspire and intrigue audiences for generations to come.

Historical Archives: Iconic Images of Billy, The Kid

In the realm of Wild West legends, one name stands out above all others: Billy, The Kid. His life was shrouded in mystery and his exploits have captivated the public for generations. From his daring escapades to his tragic demise, Billy, The Kid has become an enduring symbol of the American frontier. And at the heart of his legend lies a collection of iconic images that offer a glimpse into his extraordinary life.

The historical archives are a treasure trove for anyone fascinated by Billy, The Kid. These archives contain a wealth of photographs, each capturing a moment in time that adds to the mystique surrounding this legendary figure. From his early days as a young cowboy to his days as an outlaw, these images bring Billy, The Kid to life in a way that words alone cannot.

For the devoted fans of Billy, The Kid, these photographs are more than just images; they are pieces of history. They provide a tangible connection to a bygone era, allowing us to walk in the footsteps of this Wild West legend. Whether you're a collector of Billy, The Kid memorabilia or simply a fan of his story, these images offer a window into his world.

But the appeal of these iconic images extends beyond the realm of collectors and enthusiasts. They have inspired artists, writers, filmmakers, and musicians alike. Billy, The Kid's image has been immortalized in novels, paintings, movies, and songs, each one adding a unique perspective to his story. The power and allure of these images cannot be denied, as they continue to inspire and captivate audiences across various mediums.

For those seeking a more immersive experience, Billy, The Kid historical tours and sightseeing offer a chance to step back in time and walk the same streets that he once did. These tours take you to the very places where Billy, The Kid lived, fought, and ultimately met his fate. It's an opportunity to experience the Wild West firsthand and gain a deeper understanding of the man behind the legend.

Whether you're a history buff, an art lover, or simply someone who appreciates a good story, the historical archives of Billy, The Kid are a treasure trove waiting to be explored. They offer a glimpse into a world long gone, yet still alive in the hearts and minds of those who are captivated by the Wild West. So dive into the archives, immerse yourself in the images, and let the legend of Billy, The Kid come to life before your eyes.

Chapter 10: Billy, The Kid Music and Songs

Folklore and Ballads: Traditional Songs about Billy, The Kid

In the vast realm of Wild West legends, few figures capture the imagination quite like Billy, The Kid. This subchapter delves into the rich tapestry of folklore and ballads that have sprung up around this enigmatic outlaw, whose name continues to echo through the annals of history. From haunting melodies to toe-tapping tunes, these traditional songs provide a captivating glimpse into the life and exploits of Billy, The Kid.

Billy, The Kid's story has been immortalized in countless songs passed down through generations. These ballads transport listeners back to a time of lawlessness and adventure, painting vivid pictures of dusty saloons, daring robberies, and the relentless pursuit of justice. Whether sung around campfires or strummed on front porches, these tunes capture the spirit of the Wild West and the enduring fascination with its most notorious gunslinger.

For those who seek to fully immerse themselves in the world of Billy, The Kid, a variety of mediums offer unique perspectives. Novels and literature set in the Wild West provide in-depth character studies and explore the complex motivations that drove Billy, The Kid. Movies and documentaries bring his story to life on the silver screen, allowing audiences to witness his escapades with stunning visual detail.

Beyond books and films, the influence of Billy, The Kid extends to art, clothing, and even video games. Artists have captured his likeness in stunning paintings, capturing his rugged charm and rebellious spirit. Wild West fashion continues to inspire designers, with cowboy hats, fringed jackets, and bandanas reminiscent of Billy, The Kid's era making a stylish comeback.

For those seeking a taste of the Wild West, themed restaurants and food experiences offer a chance to indulge in the flavors of the era. From hearty frontier feasts to smoky barbecue, these establishments transport diners back to the days of cowboys and outlaws.

The appeal of Billy, The Kid also extends to music, with musicians drawing inspiration from his story to create songs that resonate with audiences. From mournful ballads to foot-stomping anthems, these melodies capture the essence of the Wild West and the enduring allure of Billy, The Kid's legend.

Finally, vintage photographs and photography provide a glimpse into the past, allowing us to witness the faces and places that shaped Billy, The Kid's world. These images offer a tangible connection to history, reminding us of the real-life individuals who played a part in this captivating story.

Whether you're a fan of Billy, The Kid, an enthusiast of Wild West memorabilia and collectibles, or simply intrigued by the allure of this iconic outlaw, exploring the folklore and ballads surrounding his legend is an enriching journey into the heart of the Wild West. Immerse yourself in the songs, stories, and experiences that keep Billy, The Kid alive in our collective memory.

Modern Melodies: Musicians and Bands Inspired by Billy

Billy the Kid, the legendary Wild West outlaw, continues to captivate the public imagination even today. His daring escapades, romanticized persona, and tragic end have inspired countless artists across various mediums. In the realm of music, many musicians and bands have drawn inspiration from Billy's story, infusing their compositions with the spirit of the Wild West.

One notable musician who found inspiration in Billy's tale is the iconic American singer-songwriter, Bob Dylan. Known for his poetic lyrics and folk-rock sound, Dylan released a song titled "Billy" in 1969. The haunting melody and introspective lyrics beautifully capture the essence of the outlaw's life, painting a vivid picture of his struggles and adventures.

In the realm of rock music, the band Bon Jovi paid homage to Billy with their hit song "Billy Get Your Guns." Released in 1990, the track combines catchy guitar riffs with powerful vocals, evoking the rebellious spirit that Billy embodied. The song's energetic rhythm and anthemic chorus make it a favorite among fans of both the band and the Wild West legend.

Country music has also embraced Billy's story, with several artists incorporating his name and exploits into their songs. Renowned country singer Marty Robbins released the classic ballad "Billy the Kid" in 1960, recounting the outlaw's life in a heartfelt and melodic manner. Similarly, Chris LeDoux's song "Billy the Kid" pays tribute to the outlaw's legacy, showcasing the enduring fascination with his legend.

Beyond individual songs, there are bands that have wholeheartedly embraced the Wild West aesthetic, crafting entire albums inspired by Billy's story. One such band is The Killers, whose album "Sam's Town" features themes of rebellion, freedom, and the American frontier. Songs like "Sam's Town" and "When You Were Young" capture the essence of Billy's world, creating a sonic landscape that transports listeners to the Wild West.

The enduring appeal of Billy the Kid is evident in the multitude of musicians and bands who continue to find inspiration in his story. Whether it's through poetic folk ballads, rocking anthems, or country ballads, these artists pay homage to the outlaw's legacy, ensuring that his legend lives on through their modern melodies.

For fans of Billy the Kid, exploring the music inspired by his life adds another dimension to their appreciation of the Wild West legend. From Bob Dylan's introspective musings to The Killers' anthemic soundscapes, these modern melodies provide a soundtrack to accompany the tales of Billy's adventures and immortalize his legacy in the hearts of the public.

Writing a Western Tune: Tips for Creating Billy, The Kid Music

Music has always played a significant role in capturing the essence and spirit of the Wild West, with its iconic cowboys, outlaws, and legendary figures like Billy, The Kid. If you're looking to create a Western tune inspired by this Wild West legend, here are some tips to help you bring Billy, The Kid's story to life through music.

1. Research and immerse yourself in Billy, The Kid's story: Before you start composing, dive deep into the history and folklore surrounding Billy, The Kid. Learn about his life, his adventures, and the landscapes he roamed. This knowledge will serve as a solid foundation for your musical composition.

2. Embrace traditional Western instruments: To capture the authentic sound of the Wild West, incorporate instruments commonly associated with Western music, such as acoustic guitars, harmonicas, fiddles, and banjos. These instruments will evoke the spirit of the era and transport listeners back to the time of Billy, The Kid.

3. Experiment with chord progressions: Western music often features simple yet evocative chord progressions. Consider using open chords like G, C, and D to create a classic Western sound. Experiment with different progressions to find the one that best reflects the mood and tone you want to convey.

4. Infuse elements of adventure and danger: Billy, The Kid's story is filled with excitement, danger, and daring escapades. Incorporate these elements into your composition by using dynamic rhythms, unexpected

chord changes, and intense melodies. Aim to capture the tension and thrill of the Wild West.

5. Blend traditional and modern sounds: While it's essential to honor the traditional Western sound, don't be afraid to add a modern twist to your composition. Experiment with incorporating elements of other genres, such as rock or folk, to create a unique and fresh take on Billy, The Kid's story.

6. Consider the narrative structure: Like any good story, a Western tune should have a narrative structure. Think about how you can convey the different aspects of Billy, The Kid's life – from his early days as an outlaw to his tragic end – through the composition's structure, dynamics, and melody.

7. Seek inspiration from existing Billy, The Kid music: Explore existing Western and Billy, The Kid-inspired music to gain inspiration and insights into the genre. Listen to classic Western film scores, folk songs, and even modern interpretations to spark your creativity and find your own unique musical voice.

By following these tips, you can embark on a musical journey that pays homage to the legendary figure of Billy, The Kid. Whether you're creating music for films, writing a song, or composing for a Western-themed event, your tune will transport listeners to the Wild West, capturing the spirit of adventure, danger, and the untamed nature of the iconic West.

Chapter 11: Billy, The Kid Themed Restaurants and Food Experiences

Western Dining: Restaurants with a Billy, The Kid Vibe

Step into the Old West and experience the thrill of the Wild West legend, Billy, The Kid, through your taste buds. In this subchapter, we explore the unique dining establishments that offer a Billy, The Kid vibe, taking you on a culinary journey back to the days of cowboys, outlaws, and saloons.

Imagine walking into a restaurant where the walls are adorned with vintage photographs of Billy, The Kid and his gang. The aroma of smoky barbeque and sizzling steaks fills the air, transporting you to a time when hearty meals were the norm. These restaurants not only offer delicious food but also capture the essence of the Wild West, giving you a truly immersive experience.

For those who collect Billy, The Kid memorabilia and collectibles, these themed restaurants are a treasure trove. From menus featuring iconic images of Billy, The Kid to collectible coasters and mugs, you can take a piece of the legend home with you. These establishments often collaborate with local artists to create exclusive artwork inspired by Billy, The Kid, which you can purchase and add to your collection.

Billy, The Kid historical tours and sightseeing enthusiasts will find these restaurants to be an ideal stop on their journey. After exploring the historical sites and landmarks associated with the legendary outlaw, you can satisfy your hunger with authentic Western cuisine. The ambiance of these establishments will transport you back in time, allowing you to truly immerse yourself in the era.

For those who appreciate Billy, The Kid art and paintings, these restaurants offer a feast for the eyes. The walls are adorned with stunning artwork that captures the spirit of the Wild West. You can admire intricate portraits of Billy, The Kid and scenes from his adventures while enjoying a delicious meal.

Not only do these restaurants cater to the visual senses, but they also indulge your auditory senses. Many of them feature live performances of Billy, The Kid-inspired music and songs, bringing the atmosphere alive. Talented musicians strumming guitars and belting out cowboy tunes will transport you to a time when music was an integral part of Western culture.

So, whether you're a fan of Billy, The Kid novels and literature, movies and documentaries, clothing and fashion, gaming and video games, photography and vintage photographs, or simply love the idea of themed restaurants and food experiences, these western dining establishments with a Billy, The Kid vibe are a must-visit. Prepare to be transported to the Wild West as you indulge in delicious food, soak in the rich history, and immerse yourself in the legend of Billy, The Kid.

Signature Dishes: Culinary Delights Inspired by Billy

In the world of Billy, The Kid, his legend lives on not only through stories and artifacts but also through the unforgettable flavors that define the Wild West. Step into the world of Billy and indulge in a culinary journey like no other. This subchapter delves into the signature dishes inspired by the man himself, offering a unique dining experience that transports you back to the era of outlaws and cowboys.

For those with a taste for adventure, Billy, The Kid themed restaurants and food experiences offer a range of delectable dishes that pay homage to the legendary figure. Sink your teeth into a mouthwatering Billy, The Kid burger, featuring a juicy patty topped with smoky bacon and tangy barbecue sauce, perfectly capturing the essence of the Wild West. Or perhaps you prefer something with a touch of spice? Try the Billy, The Kid chili, a hearty bowl of slow-cooked beef, beans, and spices that will warm your soul and make you feel like you're sitting around a campfire under the starry sky.

If you're a fan of literature and cinema, you'll appreciate the carefully curated menu at these themed restaurants. The Billy, The Kid steak, cooked to perfection and served with a side of roasted vegetables, is a nod to the hearty meals enjoyed by cowboys on their long journeys across the plains. Pair it with a glass of whiskey, just like Billy himself would have, and savor the flavors of the Old West.

For those who prefer to bring a piece of Billy, The Kid into their own kitchens, there are cookbooks available that feature recipes inspired by the era. From cowboy stews to traditional frontier desserts, these recipes allow you to recreate the flavors of the Wild West in your own home. Whip up a batch of Billy, The Kid's favorite biscuits or try your hand at making a mouthwatering cobbler using the fruits of the land.

No matter how you choose to indulge in the culinary delights inspired by Billy, The Kid, one thing is for certain – you'll be transported to a time of adventure, danger, and untamed wilderness. So gather your friends and family, and embark on a dining experience like no other, where the spirit of Billy, The Kid lives on through every bite. Let your taste buds be your guide as you savor the flavors of the Wild West and create memories that will last a lifetime.

Immersive Experiences: Themed Dinners and Events

Step back in time and immerse yourself in the thrilling world of Billy, The Kid with our exclusive themed dinners and events. As avid fans of this Wild West legend, we understand the desire to fully experience the excitement and adventure that surrounded Billy's life. That's why we have curated a series of unforgettable experiences that cater to the interests of Billy, The Kid enthusiasts from all walks of life.

Imagine stepping into a meticulously recreated 19th-century saloon, complete with swinging doors, rustic wooden interiors, and the sounds of lively piano music filling the air. Our themed dinners take you on a journey through time, allowing you to indulge in authentic Wild West cuisine while immersing yourself in the atmosphere of Billy's era. Savor mouthwatering dishes such as hearty buffalo stew, tender barbecued ribs, and freshly baked cornbread, all carefully prepared using traditional recipes from the Old West.

But our immersive experiences go beyond just dining. For those seeking a more interactive adventure, we offer thrilling events that transport you directly into the world of Billy, The Kid. Join a gang of outlaws for an action-packed treasure hunt, where you'll follow hidden clues, solve puzzles, and uncover the secrets of Billy's life. Or, if you prefer a more relaxed experience, join us on a historical tour and sightseeing adventure, where expert guides will take you to the very places Billy once roamed, sharing fascinating stories and anecdotes along the way.

For the creative souls among us, we have partnered with renowned artists and painters to offer exclusive Billy, The Kid-inspired art workshops. Learn to capture the spirit of the Wild West on canvas, guided by experts who have dedicated their careers to preserving Billy's legacy through their art. And let's not forget the captivating world of literature and film – immerse yourself in Billy, The Kid novels, movies, and documentaries that bring his legend to life in vivid detail.

Whether you're a collector of Billy, The Kid memorabilia, a fan of his music and songs, or simply someone who appreciates the fashion and style of the Wild West, our immersive experiences have something for everyone. We invite you to step into the shoes of a legend, to taste, see, and feel the essence of Billy, The Kid. Join us on this extraordinary journey and discover a world that will ignite your imagination and leave you with memories to last a lifetime.